British Reconn
Aircraft of the
1970s and '80s

CHRIS GOSS

HISTORIC MILITARY AIRCRAFT SERIES, VOLUME 10

Front cover: Seen overhead RAF Lossiemouth is Shackleton AEW.2 WL793. *Ermintrude* was grounded in 1981, after which it was used for battle damage repair but was soon towed to the fire dump and was all but destroyed and its remains cut up for scrap.

Back cover: In June 1978, Nimrod MR.1 XV262 is seen overhead RAF St Mawgan.

Title page: In November 1971, D Flt 849 Sqn was involved in a flypast over Singapore. The nearest aircraft is Gannet AEW.3 XL471/070, and alongside is Gannet AEW.3 XL481/071. XL471 ended its days at RAE Farnborough, where it was sold privately and used for spares, much of the remainder then being scrapped in 1988. XL481 first flew in May 1960 and was delivered the following month. It would be scrapped at RAF Lossiemouth in 1979. (via C. O'Connell)

Contents page: Canberra TT.18 WK123 of 100 Sqn, seen at RAF Brize Norton in September 1991, had a varied career. Delivered in 1954, it joined the RN for target towing duties, only to return to the RAF in 1987. The year after this photograph was taken, this aircraft had been put up for disposal, but, in 2007, it was reported as surviving at Manching in Germany.

Published by Key Books
An imprint of Key Publishing Ltd
PO Box 100
Stamford
Lincs PE19 1XQ

www.keypublishing.com

The right of Chris Goss to be identified as the author of this book has been asserted in accordance with the Copyright, Designs and Patents Act 1988 Sections 77 and 78.

Typeset by SJmagic DESIGN SERVICES, India.

Contents

Foreword...4

Introduction..7

Chapter 1   Canberra...8

Chapter 2   Gannet..45

Chapter 3   Nimrod...62

Chapter 4   Shackleton..78

Foreword

I was delighted to be invited to write the Foreword to this wonderful photographic record of four iconic aircraft in service with the Royal Air Force (RAF) and Royal Navy (RN), even though my flying hours were predominantly spent in the Nimrod MR.1 and MR.2.

Initially commissioned in the RAF Regiment, I had always harboured the wish to be an aircrew officer and finally was allowed to undergo navigator training at RAF Finningley in 1972. During the course, the prospect of eventually flying in a fast jet aircraft was appealing, and we were given the opportunity to see and sit in some of the aircraft. What a huge difference it was, therefore, to sample a shiny, barely 18-months-old Nimrod MR.1. Sitting in a comfortable swivelling armchair in front of the large tactical display and interacting with the routine navigator (nav) in the neighbouring seat onto whose large map table an overhead projector shone the moving position of the aircraft, my thoughts were interrupted by an Air Electronics Operator (AEOp) who asked, 'Excuse me sir, would you like a cup of coffee?' This was definitely my type of aircraft! Moreover, the crew told me that navs could be the captain of the aircraft, and some went on to be squadron commanders too.

On completion of the Nimrod OCU course at RAF St Mawgan, I was posted to 203 Sqn at RAF Luqa, in Malta, as the second nav on the crew. Many of the sensors had been carried over from the Shackleton, but any shortcomings were more than compensated by the professionalism of the operators. Maritime aircrews are traditionally organised as constituted crews, which not only helps the mentoring of the novices, as I then was, but also engenders crew pride, loyalty and a great sense of camaraderie.

At any one time, there was always a good number of Soviet submarines trying to remain undetected in the Mediterranean, but we had a good handle on their patrol areas. Overt surface surveillance sorties ranged from visiting the various anchorages that were routinely used by the Soviets, to taking copious photographs of warships as they entered the Mediterranean, having transited through the Bosphorus Straits. There were also unusual but highly enjoyable deployments, for example, to the Seychelles to participate in the flypast on their Independence Day in June 1976.

On leaving Malta in 1977, I was posted to 120 Sqn (CXX) at RAF Kinloss and, soon after arrival, achieved my goal of becoming a nav captain. The nature of maritime air operations now could not have been more different from flying in the Mediterranean. Anti-submarine warfare (ASW) sorties were more often than not the final element of integrated surveillance that would first detect Soviet submarines leaving their bases and then transit south towards their patrol areas in the Atlantic or continue their journey to the Mediterranean. Next, long-range detections would be made on the Sound Surveillance System (SOSUS) chains of underwater hydrophones filling the Greenland–Iceland–UK (GIUK) gaps. Nimrod crews were held in high states of readiness for any submarine that approached these chains, and drop patterns of passive sonobuoys to detect, localise and track the submarine. Nimrods operated in electronic covertness. Tracking a Soviet submarine might go on for several days with the handover from one Nimrod crew to another, or perhaps to or from a US Navy P3C flying out of Keflavik, Iceland, being conducted in complete radio silence by laying specific patterns of sonobuoys, which could be deciphered by the oncoming aircraft.

While many overt surface surveillance sorties were flown to intercept and gain the latest available intelligence on ships of the Soviet Navy, there was also a wide range of clandestine operations, such as monitoring merchant vessels suspected of being involved in smuggling drugs or weapons, both in UK waters and overseas. Another challenge was the monitoring of exercises conducted by the Soviet Navy in the Barents Sea. Because of their sensitivity, these covert operations were always authorised at a very high level. Nimrods also helped provide integrated search and rescue (SAR) cover 365 days a year. The saving of lives at sea was one of the most satisfying and rewarding outcomes that could be achieved by a Nimrod crew.

On 6 April 1982, 42 Sqn deployed two Nimrod MR.1s to Ascension Island to provide direct support to the Task Force heading for the Falklands. Just four weeks later, the first Nimrod MR.2P (the P signifying the fitting of an air-to-air refuelling probe) arrived and, for the next six months, Nimrods continued to provide support over greatly extended ranges in the South Atlantic.

UK-based ASW and surface surveillance operations continued throughout the1980s and my second appointment at RAF Kinloss was as a flight commander with 201 Sqn, and later, a third as the wing commander CO of CXX. However, global politics started to change, with probably the most dramatic for the Nimrod force being the Iraqi invasion of Kuwait in August 1990. I was privileged to command the first deployment of Nimrod MR.2P crews flying to Seeb, Oman, on 12 August 1990, as part of Operation *Granby*. Our task initially focused on enforcing the maritime embargo on the movement of Iraqi vessels, as part of the UK's contribution to the US-led coalition of willing nations.

The Nimrod MR.2s were progressively fitted with new sensors and capabilities, which enabled them to contribute fully to the Intelligence, Surveillance, Target Acquisition and Reconnaissance (ISTAR) order of battle for operations both over sea and land. In 1992, Nimrods at RAF St Mawgan moved to Kinloss and throughout the 1990s and into the new millennium, improved sensors and communications saw the aircraft being used more frequently in overland ISTAR operations; it was on such operations over Kandahar in September 2006 that a Nimrod MR.2P suffered an on-board fire following aerial refuelling and crashed, sadly killing all 14 members of the crew.

Of the other aircraft depicted in this book, I was fortunate enough to fly on a few 51 Sqn Nimrod R sorties in the Persian Gulf. I had previously thought the aircraft to be a strategic asset and was hugely impressed how the latest sensors and communications enabled tactical information to be used in real time. In its role of gathering electronic intelligence, it was like a huge airborne vacuum cleaner hoovering up electronic transmissions. The specialist operators onboard also conducted communications intelligence by listening to and analysing radio emissions.

While with 203 Sqn, I never had the opportunity to fly in a Canberra PR.9 of our sister squadron, 13 Sqn. Later, as a lead in to an exchange tour with the RN, I qualified as an RN Observer, but only flew in Wessex and Sea King helicopters, as the Gannets were retired in December 1978. I did, however, have an opportunity to fly in a Shackleton. The first MR.1 aircraft had entered service with CXX in April 1951. In April 1991, I was the CO of CXX and the CO of 8 Sqn, which flew the Shackleton airborne early warning (AEW), suggested we should mark the 40th anniversary of the aircraft by flying together on an AEW sortie. Accordingly, he landed at RAF Kinloss and I later joined him on board but, on take-off, a fault developed in one of the engines that necessitated our immediate return to RAF Lossiemouth; my long-anticipated flight in a Shackleton lasted less than 10 minutes!

With the last flight of the Nimrod MR.2 in May 2010, the cancellation of the Nimrod MRA.4 programme and the disbandment of the squadrons, our island nation was left without a long-range maritime patrol aircraft for ASW and surface surveillance operations, as well as no longer being effectively able to meet its commitment for SAR coverage far out into the Atlantic Ocean. The Nimrod

R.1 continued flying until June 2011 and the first of its replacement RC-135 Rivet Joint was delivered to 51 Sqn in November 2013. To my great personal delight, CXX reformed on 1 April 2018, the centenary of the formation of the RAF and 120 Sqn. It received its first Boeing Poseidon MRA.1 in Florida in October 2019 and, on 4 February 2020, flew back to Scotland. Although CXX is now based at RAF Lossiemouth, alongside the newly reformed 201 Sqn, it was most fitting that the inaugural flight should land at Kinloss, while major works at RAF Lossiemouth took a further eight months to be completed.

I commend this pictorial history as yet another valuable contribution to the history of aviation in the RN and RAF.

Air Commodore Andrew Neal AFC FRAeS

Nimrod MR.2 XV234 would become MRA.4 ZJ518, which then first flew in December 2004. Its last flight was March 2010, and within a year, it had been scrapped.

Introduction

This book is the fourth in Key Publishing's series devoted to British combat aircraft of the 1970s and 1980s, the 20 years that were destined to be the last two decades of the Cold War.

The first book in the series covered the Lightning and Phantom, the second the Buccaneer and Vulcan, while the third covered the ground-attack/tactical reconnaissance aircraft that are the Jaguar and Harrier. This book covers reconnaissance and AEW aircraft. This comprises the maritime reconnaissance and AEW Avro Shackleton, the Hawker Siddeley Nimrod – which came in many guises but mainly acted in a maritime reconnaissance role – and the venerable English Electric Canberra in reconnaissance and electronic countermeasures (ECM) roles. It will also include the specialist target towing roles performed by 7 and 100 Sqns and the Royal Navy's Fleet Requirements and Air Direction Unit (FRADU). The book also covers the Fleet Air Arm's Fairey Gannet, which, with just one squadron, carried out the Royal Navy's AEW role. All four aircraft had long careers – the Shackleton first flew in 1949 and retired in 1991, the Canberra first flew in 1949 and retired in 2006, while the Gannet also first flew in 1949 and finally retired in 1978. The relative youngster was the Nimrod, which first flew in 1967 and retired in 2011. However, this was heavily based on the de Havilland Comet airliner, which also first flew in 1949; it would appear 1949 was quite a momentous year for British aviation!

In the very early years of the 1970s, the Canberra was still just about being used in the bombing and interdiction roles, so I will make no excuses for including some photos of this. By June 1972, however, these remaining squadrons had been disbanded or converted, leaving just reconnaissance, target towing, intelligence gathering, ECM and operational training roles.

I would like to thank Air Commodore Andrew Neal, a 'Nimrod Man' and former Commanding Officer of 120 Sqn, for agreeing to write the foreword, Andy Thomas for his advice and guidance – his knowledge of such RAF matters is far greater than mine – and Andrew Brookes, who also helped with the Canberra. I would like to thank Bernd Rauchbach yet again for checking the captions for me and Chris O'Connell, a former neighbour of ours, whom I met by chance during COVID-19 vaccinating, for his photographs from his time flying in Gannets with 849 Sqn. Last but not least, this book yet again is dedicated to the late David Howley, without whose generosity I would not have had access to so many photographs of aircraft he encountered, photographed and logged during his RAF career and afterwards.

Chris Goss
Marlow 2022

Chapter 1

Canberra

Prototype Canberra B.1 VN799 first flew on 13 May 1949 and was delivered on 27 October the same year. On 18 August 1953, it was flying with the Aircraft Instrument Examinations Unit and, upon climbing out from RAF Woodbridge in Suffolk, suffered a double engine failure at 300ft. The pilot, Flight Lieutenant (Flt Lt) Harry Maule, attempted to force-land on open ground but hit trees and crashed just southeast of Sutton Heath. The pilot and the civilian flight test observer, Mike Burgan, were both injured.

Canberra PR.7 WT523 was delivered to the RAF in June 1955 and is seen here in the markings of 17 Sqn in 1967. On 25 February 1971, by then with 31 Sqn, it suffered a bird strike to the canopy and was badly damaged, landing at RAF Laarbruch. On 11 March 1971, it was assessed as suffering Category 5 damage and was then used for ground instruction duties before being burned on the RAF Laarbruch fire dump in 1976.

Photographed in August 1962, Canberra B.2 WH642 was, at that time, with C Flight (Flt) 151 Sqn. Delivered in October 1952, it was struck off charge in January 1976 and was burned at the RAF Catterick Fire Training School after that.

Canberra PR.3 WE168 served with 39 and 69 Sqns and 231 Operational Conversion Unit (OCU) before being struck off charge in May 1969, after which it ended up on the fire dump at RAF Manston in Kent. Scrapped in 1990, the cockpit was saved and is now at the Norfolk and Suffolk Aviation Museum at Flixton in Suffolk. This photograph shows it with 231 OCU.

Canberra T.4 WH861 is believed to have joined 56 (F) Sqn's Target Facilities Flight at RAF Wattisham in July 1968. Delivered in July 1953, it had previously flown with 39 Sqn in 1959 and was apparently sold as scrap at RAF St Athan in 1970, although 56 (F) Sqn's records state it left the squadron in 1975. Note 56 (F) Sqn's red and white chequerboard on the nose. The aircraft is painted pale grey.

Close up of 56 (F) Sqn's 'Firebird' badge.

Canberra WJ636 was built as a B.2 and arrived at 104 Sqn in 1954, after which it served with 61 and 35 Sqns. In October 1967, it was converted to TT.18 trainer, which was completed in March 1969. In October, the aircraft was transferred to the RN, joining the Fleet Requirements Unit (FRU) for target towing duties. In December 1972, the FRU was merged with the Air Direction Training Unit to form the Fleet Requirements and Air Direction Training Unit (FRADTU, later FRADU from 1972). It continued flying until February 1987, when it went into storage at RAF St Athan, only to rejoin the RAF a year later with 100 Sqn at RAF Wyton. It was finally grounded in January 1992 and eventually scrapped in August 1995.

WJ636 was painted pale grey overall with white bands on the wing and around the fuselage (the latter was later DayGlo red). Underneath was yellow and black.

Canberra E.15 of 100 Sqn is photographed in 1977. Built as a B.2 and delivered to 12 Sqn in 1955, this aircraft was seen at the 1958 Farnborough Airshow. It later flew with 73, 32 and 249 Sqns as part of the RAF Akrotiri Strike Wing. Converted to an E.15, it then flew with 98, 360 and 100 Sqns before being retired in 1982. It was initially on display at RAF Cosford but was scrapped in 1991; the nose section is still believed to be in a private collection in Sussex, however.

Canberra B(I).8, seen here with 16 Sqn, was delivered in December 1958 but ended its days in 1972 as a target on the Nordhorn ranges. It flew with the Station Flight RAF Wildenrath, then 88 Sqn (which was renumbered 14 Sqn in December 1961) and, from February 1965, spent much of its remaining time with 16 Sqn.

Canberra B(I).8 XM936 was delivered to the RAF in April 1959 and is seen here in the markings of 3 Sqn, which operated the Canberra from 1961 until it was disbanded at RAF Laarbruch in 1971. This aircraft was then delivered to Peru, where it served as serial 254 with the Escuadrón de Bombardeo 921 and 922.

Photographed at RAF Alconbury in July 1984 is Canberra T.17 WJ981 of 360 Sqn. Delivered to the RAF in August 1953, it would be scrapped at RAF Wyton in August 1995.

Canberra PR.7 WH798, seen here with 17 Sqn, was delivered in 1954, after which it served with 542, 100, 17, 80, 13 and 31 Sqns. It ended its days in 1971 as a ground decoy at either RAF Brüggen or Wildenrath but soon went to RAF St Athan for storage. It was sold in 1981, and much of it was cut up. What remained was obtained by the Wales Aircraft Museum, however, on that museum's demise, it was scrapped in 1992. The nose survived and is now with the Suffolk Aviation Heritage Group at Kesgrave.

Canberra PR.7 WH775, seen here with 31 Sqn, ended its days with 13 Sqn at RAF Wyton, after which it was scrapped. The nose remains and is in private hands in Wales.

The history of Canberra PR.3 WE139 is well known. In August 1953, it was delivered to 540 Sqn as part of the New Zealand Air Race Flight, and on 8–9 October 1953, flown by Flt Lt Monty Burton and Flt Lt Don Gannon, it flew from Heathrow Airport to Harewood International Airport in New Zealand in an elapsed time of 23hr, 50min and 42sec, setting a new world record in the process. In 1954, it joined 69 Sqn, then 39 Sqn and joined 231 OCU in December 1962. Its last flight was to RAF Henlow in April 1969, and the following year it went to the RAF Museum at Hendon. This photograph shows it with 231 OCU.

Canberra PR.9 XH134, seen here with 1 Photographic Reconnaissance Unit (PRU) at RAF Alconbury in August 1990, served with 13, 58 and 39 (1 PRU) Sqns before being retired in July 2006. It was then flown to Kemble Airfield and privately purchased and, after restoration and modification in 2013, was flying again with the civilian registration G-OHMD. In 2016, this aircraft was put up for auction by Bonhams and was later bought privately and now resides at Cotswold Airport, formerly Kemble Airfield.

The badge of 51 Sqn is seen on the tail of an unidentified Canberra B.6, photographed in November 1982. 51 Sqn, then based at RAF Wyton, operated this variant of Canberra until October 1976, so it is assumed that this aircraft has been grounded.

Canberra PR.9 XH170 joined the RAF in 1960 and spent nearly all of its life with 39 Sqn both at RAF Luqa and RAF Wyton. When its flying career was over, it became the gate guardian at RAF Wyton.

Canberra T.17 WJ630/ED of 360 Sqn is seen at RAF Mildenhall in May 1989. It was built as a B.2 in 1954 and served with 100 and 45 Sqns before being loaned to the Royal New Zealand Air Force (RNZAF), where it flew with 75 Sqn. On its return, it was converted to a T.17, which was completed by 1967, later joining 360 Sqn. Six years after these photographs were taken, it was scrapped.

Canberra T.17A WJ607of 360 Sqn is seen at RAF Upper Heyford in May 1990. Built in 1953, it was retired, still in flying condition, and joined the British Civil Register in December 1994. It was then bought by Mike Beachyhead's Thunder City collection, based in South Africa, and in August 1995, it was registered ZU-AUE. On 30 September 1995, it took off from Cape Town International Airport on a test flight, but in the vicinity of Yzerfontaine, Western Cape, it turned inland, went into a spin and crashed, killing both members of the crew.

Canberra PR.9 XH168 of 39 Sqn is photographed at RAF Mildenhall in August 1980. Built in 1960, it joined 59 Sqn, then 39 and 13 Sqns and, finally, 39 Sqn (with a short spell with the Aeroplane and Armament Experimental Establishment [A&AEE]). It went into storage in 1981, before joining 1 PRU and then 39 Sqn. On 8 September 2003, this aircraft, still with 39 Sqn, suffered a landing accident at RAF Marham, bursting both main wheels, after which the starboard undercarriage leg broke away and the aircraft swung off the runway. The aircraft was not repaired, and, after being used for spares, it was scrapped in July 2005.

Canberra PR.7 WH794, seen at RAF Abingdon in September 1980, was delivered to the RAF in 1954, after which it was known to have served with 58 Sqn in 1962 and was with 13 Sqn at RAF Luqa in the 1970s. By the time this photograph was taken, it was being used for ground instruction, and, in 1984, it went to the RAF Catterick Fire Training School, where it was burnt.

Canberra PR.7 WJ825 of 13 Sqn is seen at a wet RAF Akrotiri in December 1979. Built in 1954, it too ended its days at the RAF Catterick Fire Training School, and, by October 1985, it had been totally destroyed.

This unusual Canberra PR.7 WH774, photographed at RAF Greenham Common in June 1979, was flying with the Ministry of Technology and loaned to the Radar Research Flying Unit at Pershore Airfield in Worcestershire, which had another two Canberras, WJ646 and WK163. WH774 had been modified to collect infrared signatures from ship targets and conducted trials for the Red Top missile and Decca Navigator system. It was reported as being on the dump at Royal Aircraft Establishment (RAE) Farnborough in 1994 and had been scrapped by 1995.

Overhead RAF Greenham Common in June 1979 is Canberra PR.9 XH167 of 39 Sqn. Built in 1960, in October 1982 it joined the Chilean Air Force with the serial 342. This aircraft was destroyed in a crash near Punta Arenas on 25 May 1983.

Coming into land at RAF Greenham Common in June 1979 is Canberra PR.7 WJ817 of 13 Sqn. Built in 1954, it flew with 58, 17, 80 and finally 13 Sqns before being used for battle damage repair at RAF Wyton from 1981 onwards. However, in 1989, it appeared on the fire dump and by 1995 had been scrapped.

Seen at RAF Luqa in July 1978 is Canberra PR.9 XH174 of 39 Sqn. Delivered in 1960, it was reported as being in store at RAF St Athan in 1989. The cockpit section survived, being sold in 2006. In 2009, it was in private hands in Staffordshire, and it was last noted at Welshpool in 2017. This aircraft was reported as being the first to be seen fitted with a fin-mounted ECM pod.

Awaiting an eventual fate at RAF St Athan in August 1977 is Canberra PR.7 WT507, with the 31 Sqn badge visible on the tail. Although scrapped, the nose section survived and went to 384 (Mansfield) Sqn Air Training Corps (ATC).

Another Canberra PR.7 seen at RAF St Athan in August 1977 was WT534 in 17 Sqn markings. Built in 1954, it first flew with 17 Sqn, then 80 Sqn and then back to 17 Sqn. Shortly after this photograph was taken, it went to RAF Halton, where it was used for ground instruction until 1981, when it ended up on RAF Halton's fire dump. Broken up the following year, the nose section survived, first going to RAF Abingdon, then 489 (Acocks Green and Olton) Sqn ATC in Birmingham and then in 1984 to 492 (Solihull) Sqn ATC. It was then at the Doncaster Aeroventure Museum, but, in 2019, it was reported as being up for sale and is now owned by the Vulcan to the Sky Trust.

The 13 Sqn badge is visible on the tail of Canberra PR.7 WJ825 during the Queen's Jubilee Review at RAF Finningley in July 1977. It ended up at the RAF Catterick Fire Training School and had been totally burnt by October 1985.

Another participant at the Queen's Jubilee Review was Canberra PR.9 XH174 of 39 Sqn. The cockpit section survived, being sold in 2006, and it was last recorded as being in private hands in Welshpool in 2017.

A close-up of the 39 Sqn badge on the tail of Canberra PR.9 XH174 at RAF Finningley in July 1977.

Photographed at RAF Akrotiri, while employed on target towing for the Armament Practice Camps, is Canberra WT509 of 100 Sqn. Delivered in 1955, it flew in the reconnaissance role with 13, 17, 80 and 58 Sqns before going to 100 Sqn in 1991 and then back to 1 PRU. It was then used for spares at RAF Marham and, in 2004, was broken up for scrap.

Canberra TT.18 WK122 of 7 Sqn is seen at RAF St Mawgan. It began life as a B.2 in 1954, serving with 15 Sqn. It was sold to the British Aircraft Corporation (BAC) in 1981 and then sold to Flambards Theme Park in Cornwall in 1988. Scrapped in 2000 because it had become unsafe, the cockpit section is now in private hands in Cumbria.

The task of training Canberra aircrew was undertaken by 231 OCU. This photograph shows Canberra T.4s WT483 and WH919. WT483 entered service in 1955 with 69 Sqn before moving to 231 OCU at RAF Bassingbourne, then to 39 Sqn at RAF Wyton and finally back to 231 OCU. Sold to BAC in 1981, it then moved to Filton in 1986 and was finally sold to the Stratford Aircraft Collection in 1989. In 2010, it was bought by Malta Air Services and is now alongside air traffic control at Malta Luqa International Airport. WH919 was badly damaged in a taxiing accident at RAF Cottesmore on 12 November 1975 while still with 231 OCU, and although it went for repairs, it was declared a write off. It was struck off charge in January 1976 and scrapped at RAF Aldergrove.

Canberra T.4 WT480 of 231 OCU is at RAF Abingdon in September 1986. Delivered in 1955, in March 1996 it went into storage at RAF Shawbury, only to be scrapped in 2005. The cockpit section survived and is now at the Flugplatzmuseum at Gütersloh in Germany.

Canberra B.2 WJ637, seen here with 231 OCU, last flew in September 1982, having first joined 35 Sqn in 1954. It was then located outside Trenchard Hall at RAF College Cranwell and painted as WH699 and named *Aries IV. Aries IV* had been the holder of numerous records in 1953–55 but had been destroyed in an accident near RAF Strubby on 28 November 1959. WJ637 was then dismantled in 1995 and had been scrapped in Essex by February 1996.

Another 231 OCU Canberra B.2 was WJ677. It was first flown in 1955, and after its service life came to an end, its nose section went on display at the Fleet Air Arm Museum in Yeovilton. It is now believed to be in private hands in Cornwall.

Canberra T.4 WH849 of 231 OCU is seen at RAF Fairford in July 1991. Delivered in 1955, it became the oldest T.4 flying with the RAF. It was flown by RAF Marham, Coningsby and Binbrook Station Flts, RAE, 231 OCU, 76, 85, 360, 100, 7 and 39 Sqns. In 2002, it went into storage at RAF Shawbury to be sold in 2005, after which it was scrapped. The nose section can now be seen at the museum at former RAF Laarbruch in Germany.

Canberras were also used by the RAE. Canberra T.4 WJ992 was built as a B.2 and went to 76 Sqn in October 1953. It left the RAF in January 1957, after which it was converted to a T.4. It then flew with the Blind Landing Experimental Unit at Martlesham Heath in Suffolk. Then, in 1962, it joined the Royal Radar Establishment (RRE) at Pershore in Worcestershire and, then in 1977, joined the Aerospace Research Squadron at RAE Bedford. Its flying days over, it was seen deteriorating at Hurn Airport for a number of years, after which it was scrapped. The nose section is now in private hands in South Wales.

Canberra TT.18 WK123 of 100 Sqn, seen at RAF Brize Norton in September 1991, had a varied career. Delivered in 1954, it joined the RN's FRU for target towing duties, only to return to the RAF in 1987. The year after this photograph was taken, this aircraft had been put up for disposal, but in 2007 it was reported as surviving at Manching in Germany.

Canberra T.17 WD955 was built as a B.2 and delivered to 101 Sqn in 1951. It then went to 617, 21, 245 and 98 Sqns before being converted to a T.17 in 1964. It then joined 360 Sqn, until it was gifted to the Norsk Luftfahartmuseum at Bodø in Norway in 1995. This photograph was taken in June 1990, while the aircraft was still with 360 Sqn.

Photographed in August/September 1979 is Canberra B.6 XH567. Built in 1955, it went directly to the Ministry of Aircraft. After this, it flew with the RAE, Air Torpedo Development Unit and RRE before being flown to the RAE at Bedford in December 1976. Having been prepared by Delta Jets, it left Kemble Airfield in April 1998 headed for Air Platforms Inc at Lakeport, California, where it was given the serial N40UP and used for upper atmosphere mapping work. It last flew in 2015 and was reported as being up for sale by auction in October 2020.

Canberra TT.18 WK118 of 100 Sqn is photographed at RAF Fairford in July 1989. Delivered in 1954, it was grounded in 1991 and later scrapped, but the nose section can be seen today at the Avro Heritage Museum at Woodford.

Another Canberra T.17A of 360 Sqn was WH646, seen here at Fairford in July 1987. Built as a B.2 in 1952, it served with 50, 10 and 45 Sqns before being loaned to the RNZAF in 1958–62; it was flown by 75 Sqn from Tengah, Singapore, on anti-terrorist operations during the Malayan Emergency. Returned to the RAF, it flew with 45 Sqn, after which it was converted to a T.17 and, from 1967, flew with 360 Sqn. Flying days over, it was scrapped, but its nose section is on display at the Midland Air Museum at Baginton, Coventry.

Seen at RAF Cottesmore in November 1974 is Canberra T.4 WT488 of 231 OCU. Delivered in 1955, it was later sold to BAC, and it was last seen on the dump at Dunsfold Airfield in Surrey in 1999, being scrapped after that.

Canberra TT.18 WJ680 of 100 Sqn, seen at RAF St Mawgan in August 1986, was delivered to 104 Sqn as a B.2 in 1955, subsequently going to 105 Sqn and then 59 Sqn. By 1968, it had been converted to a TT.18. On 7 December 1972, and now with 7 Sqn, the rudder top hinge sheared off in an air test. The navigator, Pilot Officer (Plt Off) Geoff Burns, ejected successfully and the pilot, Flt Lt Dave Burgess, carried out a successful wheels-up landing, for which he was awarded the Air Force Cross. The aircraft took nearly three years to be repaired, after which it went to 100 Sqn and later into storage in 1991. It was sold in 1999, becoming registered as G-BURM, and in 2002 was ferried to Temora Aviation Museum, Canberra, where it became VH-ZSQ. Flying until June 2010, considerable restoration was then carried out, and it returned to the air on 28 June 2021.

Photographed at RAF Greenham Common in July 1983 is Canberra T.4 WJ879 of 231 OCU. Built in 1955, this aircraft would be scrapped at RAF Wyton in December 1992.

Another view of 100 Sqn's Canberra TT.18 WJ680, seen again at RAF Greenham Common in July 1983. This is the aircraft now flying in Australia.

Canberra PR.9 XH165 of 1 PRU at RAF Brize Norton in June 1984. The nose of this aircraft was last reported as being in private hands in Suffolk.

Seen at Royal Naval Air Station (RNAS) Yeovilton in September 1984 is FRADU's Canberra TT.18 WJ574. Built as a B.2 in 1953, it first joined the photo reconnaissance 540 Sqn for crew training but then moved to 57 Sqn. Sold to BAC in 1969, in 1974 it was converted to be a TT.18, joining FRADU in October 1974. In 1993, it was placed up for disposal and sold to an American buyer, who flew it to California in May 1994. It is currently at the Valiant Air Command Warbird Museum at Titusville, Florida, still in FRADU colours.

Another FRADU Canberra TT.18 seen at RNAS Yeovilton in September 1984 was WE122. Built as a B.2 in 1952, it flew with 231 OCU and 245 and 98 Sqn before going into storage, after which it joined the RN in 1971. It was then converted to be a TT.18 and joined FRADU in June 1974. Withdrawn from service in 1987, it went into storage and was offered for disposal in 1990. Broken up at RAF St Athan, the cockpit section survived and is now believed to be in a private collection in Suffolk.

Another FRADU Canberra was T.22 WT510. Built as a PR.7 in 1954, it flew with 80 and 31 Sqns before transferring to the RN in 1971. Converted to a T.22, it joined the FRADTU in March 1974 and continued flying until 1985. It was scrapped in 1991, the cockpit section surviving until 1993, when it too was scrapped.

Left and below: Getting airborne is Canberra TT.18 WK142 of FRADU at RNAS Yeovilton in July 1982. Built as a B.2 in 1954, it flew with 115, 207, 90 and 98 Sqns before going into storage. It then joined the FRU in September 1969 and, in 1972, began to be converted to a TT.18. It returned to flying in 1974 and joined the FRADU in March 1975. In 1992, it went into storage and the following year was put up for auction. It was later sold to an American collector and, in 1995, flew to Arizona. It is now believed to be at the Pima Air & Space Museum, Tucson, Arizona.

Overhead RNAS Yeovilton in July 1982 is Canberra T.22 WH803. Intended to be a PR.3, it was upgraded to be a PR.7 on the production line and joined 540 Sqn in June 1954. In 1969, it went into storage before joining the RN in 1971, after which it was converted to be a T.22 and, after a short loan to 39 Sqn, joined the FRADU in July 1976. In 1984, it went into storage at RAF St Athan and in 1991 was offered for disposal. Soon cut up, it had been totally scrapped by 1993.

Seen at RAF Alconbury in August 1982 is Canberra TT.18 WK124 of 100 Sqn. Built as a B.2, it served with 103, 59 and 213 Sqn before going into storage prior to being converted to a TT.18. In 1991, it was delivered to RAF Manston for crash rescue training. In 2000, it was recorded as being at the Jet Age Museum at Gloucester, but the fuselage is now stated as being at the Cornwall Aviation Heritage Centre, Newquay.

Seen overhead RAF Odiham in September 1982, a Canberra TT.18 of 100 Sqn shows off its distinctive lines.

Seen at RAF St Mawgan in August 1980 is Canberra TT.18 WK124 of 7 Sqn. The fuselage is now believed to be at the Cornwall Aviation Heritage Centre, Newquay.

On the nose of Canberra TT.18 WJ721 of 7 Sqn, pictured at RAF St Mawgan in August 1980, are the arms of Truro. The motto translates as 'The horn is exalted in God'. Built as a B.2, it was modified to be a TT.18 and was broken up in 1988, although the nose section was saved, and now, in 15 Sqn markings, it can be seen at the Morayvia Museum, Kinloss.

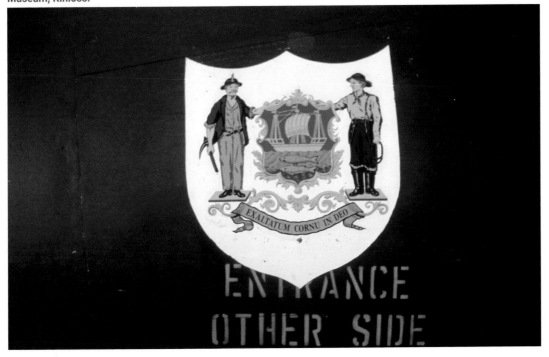

Seen landing at RAF Lossiemouth is Canberra B.2 WH 667 of 100 Sqn. On 7 November 1980, an engine on this aircraft blew up on take-off from RAF Akrotiri. It then rolled, hit the ground and burst into flames. Sadly, neither of the crew survived.

A Canberra PR.7 of 13 Sqn is getting airborne from RAF Luqa in July 1978. 13 Sqn had moved from RAF Akrotiri to Malta in October 1972 and would move to RAF Wyton in October 1978, disbanding in January 1982.

The 7 Sqn badge is seen on the tail of Canberra TT.18 WJ680 during the Queen's Jubilee Review at RAF Finningley in July 1977. After an eventful RAF career, this aircraft is now flying in Australia.

100 Sqn's distinctive badge is seen on Canberra E.15 WH964. Built as a B.6 in 1955, it became a B.15 and then an E.15. It last flew in February 1982, after which it was used for ground instruction at RAF Cosford. Disposed of in 1991, the cockpit has been in a private collection at Chailey Green, East Sussex, Bruntingthorpe and the Southampton Hall of Aviation.

A final Canberra tail at the Jubilee Review was Canberra T.17 WF890 of 360 Sqn. Built in 1952 as a B.2, it was one of six aircraft that took part in Project *Swifter* at El Adem in 1960, a joint Farnborough and Boscombe Down venture to investigate effects on airframe (and aircrew) of high-speed, low-level flight. It would be scrapped at RAF Wyton in 1995.

The old and the new – Canberra T.17 WJ630 of 360 Sqn, alongside Tornado GR.1 ZA614, RAF Abingdon, in September 1982. WJ630 would be scrapped in 1995, while ZA614, which had been delivered in July 1982, would be upgraded to a GR.4 and now sits outside the Station HQ at RAF Marham.

A sad sight. Canberras parked up at Salmesbury in 1971 awaiting either modification or disposal. To the right is Canberra B.16 WT306, which was delivered in 1955 as a B.6 and flew with 139 and 6 Sqns before being converted to a B.16, then flying with 249 Sqn and the RAF Akrotiri Strike Wing. It was sold to BAC in 1969 and then scrapped in 1976. The Akrotiri Strike Wing badge, a pink flamingo and a white lightning bolt above water, is on the tail of this aircraft, while the 249 Sqn elephant badge can be seen on the next aircraft. The latter squadron disbanded in February 1969. Two aircraft have the 213 Sqn wasp badge on the tail, this squadron being disbanded in December 1969.

RAF Canberra Variants

Canberra B.1
This was the prototype. Four were built in total.

Canberra B.2
The first production version of this aircraft. It was built for a bomber role.

Canberra B.6
This version was based on B.5, which was the prototype of the second generation of Canberra.

Canberra B(I).8
This was the first of the third generation of Canberra. It was derived from the B.6 and used for interdiction roles.

Canberra B.16
An upgraded B.6.

Canberra E.15
B.15 conversion with enhanced electronics fitted.

Canberra PR.3
The initial photo reconnaissance Canberra, which was based on the B.2.

Canberra PR.7
Photo reconnaissance variant, which was based on the B.6.

Canberra PR.9
Photo reconnaissance variant, which was based on the B(I).8.

Canberra T.4
First trainer variant, which was based on the B.2.

Canberra T.17
Early warning training variant, which was converted from the B.2.

Canberra T.17A
Improved T.17.

Canberra TT.18
Target tug conversion of the B.2.

Canberra T.22
Conversion of the PR.7 for RN use to train Buccaneer navigators.

Canberra RAF Operational Squadrons

Note: Some squadrons began or ended their use of the Canberra outside the scope of this book. As such, the years served within the time frame have been listed.

Squadron	Years Active During 1970–89
3 Sqn	until Dec 1971
7 Sqn	May 1970–Jan 1982
13 Sqn	until Jan 1982
14 Sqn	until Jun 1970
16 Sqn	until Jun 1972
31 Sqn	until Mar 1971
39 Sqn/1 PRU	from Jun 1982 (disbanded Jul 2006)
45 Sqn	until Feb 1970
51 Sqn	until Oct 1976
81 Sqn	until Jan 1970
98 Sqn	until Feb 1976
100 Sqn	from Feb 1972 (disbanded Dec 1991)
360 Sqn	until Oct 1994
231 OCU/Canberra Standardisation Flight	served throughout (disbanded Apr 1993)

Chapter 2

Gannet

Right: Two Gannet AEW.3s of 849 Sqn are seen flying over an anchored line of RN and Royal Fleet Auxiliary vessels, which includes a commando carrier, amphibious assault ship and an Oberon-class submarine. The date is unknown (probably late 1960s), but the location is presumed to be Lyme Bay.

Below: Gannet AEW.3 XL497 first flew in November 1960, after which it was assigned to 849 HQ Flt at RNAS Culdrose. It went to the Far East in January 1966, serving on board HMS *Ark Royal* and HMS *Eagle* with 849 C Flt. In August 1968, XL497 returned to the UK, still flying with 849 Sqn, at Culdrose, Brawdy ('BY' on the tail indicates Brawdy, which was 849 Sqn's base between 1964 and 1966), Yeovilton and Lossiemouth, as well as returning to HMS *Ark Royal*. Following being struck off charge, in December 1978 it became the gate guardian at HMS *Gannet*, which is a forward base located at Prestwick Airport in Ayrshire. In December 2006, it was bought by the Dumfries and Galloway Aviation Museum, where it still resides.

Gannet AEW.3 XL496, the sister aircraft to XL497, was also delivered to 849 Sqn. This photograph shows it as being based at RNAS Culdrose. It was scrapped at RAF Lossiemouth in 1979.

For the movement of high-priority freight, personnel and mail, each aircraft carrier usually housed a Carrier Onboard Delivery (COD) aircraft, a task performed by the Gannet between 1960 and 1970. Five AS.4s (XA430, XA454, XA466, XA470 and XG790) were modified for the role, with one attached to each operational seagoing 849 Sqn Flt. When within range, COD aircraft would fly ashore and collect or deliver small high-priority spares and mail in the bomb bay or in small under wing panniers, as well as personnel if it had room. XA454, seen here with 'H' for HMS *Hermes* on the tail, was delivered in November 1956 and was finally destroyed in RNAS Yeovilton's fire dump in 1981.

Another photograph of Gannet AEW.3 XL496, now with the fleet number 765, clearly showing the radome of the AN/APS-20F search radar.

Gannet ECM.6 XG797 can be seen today at the Imperial War Museum at Duxford. Built as an AS.4, it joined the RN in April 1957 but did not join 810 Sqn until May 1959. It then joined 700 Sqn at RNAS Yeovilton in August 1960, but, between November 1963 to March 1965, it was converted to an ECM.6 and then joined 831 Sqn at RAF Watton. One year later, it was being used as a ground instructional aircraft at RNAS Arbroath. Another year later, it had gone to RNAS Brawdy and joined HQ Flt of 849 Sqn, where 'BY' was applied to the tail and '766' to the nose. However, in May 1972, it went to Duxford and now wears the markings of 831 Sqn and has the numbers '277' on the nose.

Gannet AEW.3 XL450 first flew in January 1959 and was delivered to the RN three months later. It is seen here in the markings of 849 Sqn at RNAS Yeovilton in June 1976. In 1978, it was being used for ground instruction at RAF Brüggen in Germany, and, six years later, it was being stored at Bruntingthrorpe. In 1985, the aircraft was acquired by Air Classic at Mönchengladbach, but it is now at the Flugausstellung Peter Junior at Hermeskeil, Germany, in the same markings.

A nose view of Gannet AEW.3 of 849 Sqn at RNAS Yeovilton in June 1976, showing similar distinctive markings.

By comparison, Gannet AEW.3 XL502 of 849 Sqn's HQ Flt, seen here at RNAS Yeovilton in June 1977, shows few markings. Joining the RN in March 1961, a year after this photograph was taken, it was being used for ground instructional duties at RNAS Lossiemouth. It then moved to RAF Leuchars, which is where the author remembers seeing it in 1982. Struck off charge four years later, it was restored to flying condition and flew at air shows from 1987 to 1989, with the registration G-BMYP. It was then stored at Carlisle and Sandtoft, before being acquired by the Yorkshire Air Museum at Elvington; it can still be seen there today, in the markings of 849 Sqn.

Looking worse for wear at RNAS Yeovilton in October 1977 is Gannet T.5 XG883. First flown in May 1957, it did not enter service until March 1960, when it joined the Station Flt at RNAS Culdrose, joining 849 Sqn later that year. It then moved with 849 Sqn to RNAS Brawdy and was retired in January 1970, going into storage at Yeovilton before going to the Fleet Air Arm Museum, which loaned it to the Wales Air Museum at Cardiff Airport in 1983. When this museum closed in 1996, it went on loan to the Museum of Berkshire Aviation at Woodley, where it is still today.

Above and left: Seen getting airborne on HMS *Ark Royal* in 1978 is Gannet AEW.3 XL471 of 849 Sqn. It carried the numerals '043' on the nose and 'R' for *Ark Royal* on the tail. First flying in 1959 and being delivered in 1960, it ended up at RAE Farnborough. From there, it was sold privately and used for spares, the vast majority of the airframe being scrapped at Lichfield in 1988.

A good view of Gannet AEW.3 XL449 of 849 Sqn at RNAS Yeovilton in September 1975. Delivered in November 1959, it had joined 849 Sqn at RNAS Culdrose in August 1962. By the time this photograph was taken, it was flying from RNAS Lossiemouth, hence the 'LM' on the tail. Its last flight was to the Wales Air Museum in September 1978. Broken up at Cardiff in 1996, the cockpit section survived and today is in private hands in Surrey.

Gannet AEW.3 XL449 of 849 Sqn taxies out at RNAS Yeovilton in September 1976.

Gannet AEW.3 XL449 of 849 Sqn is overhead RNAS Yeovilton in September 1976.

Gannet T.2 XA508 is the only one of its type still in existence. First flown in February 1955, it was retired for ground instructional use two years and two months later. In 1975, it came to the Fleet Air Arm Museum, this photograph being taken at RNAS Yeovilton in September 1976. In 1982, it went to the Midlands Air Museum at Coventry Airport, where it still can be found today.

Starboard side of Gannet T.2 XA508, photographed a year later. It served with 737 Sqn at RNAS Eglinton, that base's shore code being 'GN', which is seen on the tail.

Gannets worked alongside other nation's aircraft. This is Gannet AEW.3 XL472 of B Flt 849 Sqn, which had been operating from HMS *Ark Royal*, seen here at RNAS Yeovilton in June 1977. It was grounded the following year, after which it was used for ground instruction at Boscombe Down. It later went to the Peter Vallance Collection at Charlwood, later moving again to the South Wales Aviation Museum at St Athan, where it can still be seen awaiting restoration.

XL472 has been 'zapped' by VAQ-33, the US Navy's electronic warfare squadron known as the 'Firebirds'.

Also seen at RNAS Yeovilton in June 1977 was Gannet AEW.3 XL450, also of B Flt 849 Sqn. This aircraft has a more impressive 'zap' from VAW-126, the US Navy's carrier-borne early warning squadron, which operated the E-2 Hawkeye aircraft. XL450 still exists at Flugausstellung Peter Junior at Hermeskeil, Germany, in the same markings.

It would appear that the US Navy spent much time and attention decorating B Flt 849 Sqn's Gannet AEW.3s in 1977. This is XL471, which had a new badge on the fuselage.

The massive badge is that of RVAW-120, the US Navy's Atlantic Fleet Replacement Squadron, which was equipped with the E-2 Hawkeye. Known as the 'Greyhawks', this unit is still operational.

Although technically outside the scope of this book, Gannet AS.1 WN344 is shown at the Royal Canadian Air Force's Central Experimental and Proving Establishment at Namao, Alberta, in June 1954. Delivered five months previously, in July 1957, it went to RNAS Arbroath, where it was used for ground instructional duties before being scrapped.

Seen coming into land is Gannet COD.4 XA466 of 849 Sqn at RNAS Lossiemouth. Built as an AS.4, it was delivered in March 1957 and soldiered on until December 1978, when it went to the Facility for Airborne Atmospheric Measurements at Cranfield in Bedfordshire. It went into storage nine years later, but it is currently on display at the Fleet Air Arm Museum.

Seen at Biggin Hill in June 1971 is Gannet XL496 of 849 Sqn. It is in the process of shutting down and folding its wings.

Right: The tail of Gannet AEW.3 XP225 of 849 Sqn, RNAS Lossiemouth. It first flew in February 1962, and in December 1971, it went into storage at Lossiemouth before being struck off charge the following month, after which it was broken up for spares.

Below: The distinctive spinner and tail markings identifies Gannet AEW.3 XP226 as belonging to 849 Sqn. First flown in March 1962, it became an instructional airframe at RNAS Lee-on-the-Solent and then the gate guardian at HMS *Dryad*, before going to the Newark Air Museum in 1982, where it still resides today.

A head-on view of Gannet AEW.3 XL449 of 849 Sqn, RNAS Yeovilton, in September 1975.

Gannet T.5 XT752, seen here at Biggin Hill in September 1971, has quite a history. Built in 1954 as a T.2, it was destined for the Indonesian Navy. However, it instead stayed in UK and was given the civilian registration G-APYO, being used by Fairey to train Indonesian Navy aircrew at White Waltham Airfield in Berkshire. It rejoined the RN in 1965, serving with 849 Sqn at RNAS Brawdy and Lossiemouth. It was reputed to be the last Gannet to land on HMS *Ark Royal* in 1978 and the last to be retired from service later that same year. The RN kept it in good condition, and it was subsequently sold to the Amjet Aircraft Museum in 1994. When the museum closed in 1996, it was bought privately in 2003, after which it was subject to legal disputes that dragged on until 2014. During this time, it was flown by cargo aircraft to Minneapolis and then by road to Richmond, Maryland, where restoration began after which the aircraft was displayed. As of May 2021, it was reported as being sold to a new owner in the US.

Getting airborne from HMS *Eagle* off the Australian coast in August 1971 is Gannet AEW.3 XP226/073 of D Flt 849 Sqn. This aircraft can be seen today at the Newark Air Museum. (via C. O'Connell)

Gannet AEW.3 XP226/073 of D Flt 849 Sqn is seen approaching Sydney in August 1971. (via C. O'Connell)

Three months later, D Flt 849 Sqn was involved in a flypast over Singapore. The nearest aircraft is Gannet AEW.3 XL471/070, and alongside is Gannet AEW.3 XL481/071. XL471 ended its days at RAE Farnborough, where it was sold privately and used for spares, much of the remainder then being scrapped in 1988. XL481 first flew in May 1960 and was delivered the following month. It would be scrapped at RAF Lossiemouth in 1979. (via C. O'Connell)

Gannets of 849 Sqn, prior to launching from HMS *Eagle*, in January 1972. This was the final departure of the Gannets, the last RN fixed-wing aircraft at that time, from the ship prior to the *Eagle*'s arrival in Portsmouth and eventual decommissioning. Once airborne, the five aircraft, four AEW.3s (XL471/070, XL491/071, XL480/072 and XP226/073) and one AS.4 COD (XA439/074), did a flypast over the ship. (via C. O'Connell)

Gannet AEW.3 XL471 of 849 Sqn is about to get airborne from HMS *Eagle* off the coast at Portsmouth in January 1972. (via C. O'Connell)

Fairey Gannet Variants
Gannet AS.1
Anti-submarine aircraft. In total, 183 were built.

Gannet T.2
Dual control trainer version of the AS.1. Thirty-eight were built.

Gannet AEW.3
Airborne early warning variant. Forty-four were built.

Gannet AS.4
Anti-submarine aircraft. There were 75 built.

Gannet COD.4
The Carrier Onboard Delivery variant, which as converted from the AS.4. Six were built.

Gannet T.5
Dual control trainer version of the AS.4. Eleven were built, three of which were converted from T.2 specification.

Gannet ECM.4/6
Electronic countermeasures aircraft. Nine were built.

Gannet Operational Units
The only operational Gannet unit during the period covered by this book was 849 Sqn, which operated the AEW.3 (until 1978) and COD.4 (until 1974).

Chapter 3

Nimrod

Seen at RAF Kinloss in the winter of 1974 is Nimrod MR.1 XV228, with the markings of 203 Sqn on the tail. It would be upgraded to an MR.2 and then was converted to an MRA.4 and given the serial ZJ523. However, when this conversion project was cancelled in October 2010, this aircraft was scrapped at Woodford the following February.

Overshooting RAF Chivenor in August 1972 is Nimrod MR.1 XV252. This was upgraded to an MR.2 and later withdrawn from service in 2010, after which it was stored at RAF Kinloss and then broken up the following year. The forward fuselage still exists in private hands in Scotland.

Nimrod MR.1 XV259, seen here at RAF St Mawgan, was converted to an AEW.3. However, following the project's cancellation, it was sold in 1991 and then broken up in 1998. The nose, minus the bulbous radome, was purchased privately in 1998 and then went to the Solway Aviation Museum, Carlisle, but is now in private hands in Wales.

Nimrod MR.1 XV246 was converted to an MR.2 but then scrapped in January 2011. On the tail is 203 Sqn's seahorse badge, which was known affectionately as 'Percy the Seahorse'. This squadron was equipped with the Nimrod MR.1 and based at RAF Luqa in Malta from October 1971, until the squadron was disbanded in December 1977.

The outer intake blank seems to indicate that this aircraft is Nimrod MR.1 XV233, which came into service in 1969. It would be upgraded to an MR.2 in the mid-1970s and then became MRA.4 with the serial ZJ520. When the MRA.4 project was cancelled, this aircraft was scrapped in February 2011. However, the inner intake blank appears to be XV246 or XV248.

The Nimrod owed its lineage to the de Havilland Comet. This is Comet C.4 XR396 of 216 Sqn. It joined the RAF in March 1962, and in August 1975 it joined Dan-Air, where it received the registration G-BDIU. In October 1980, it was grounded at Lasham in Hampshire and scrapped the following year. The nose section was saved and went to RAF Kinloss, but this too was later scrapped.

Seen at RAF Brize Norton in June 1986 is Nimrod MR.2 XV229, which at that time was based at RAF St Mawgan. Built as an MR.1, it was converted to an MR.2, and, on 26 May 2010, it was the last of its type to fly. Its final flight was from RAF Kinloss to Manston Airport in Kent, where it joined the Defence Fire Services Central Training Establishment to be used for passenger evacuation training. In 2020, the aircraft was purchased privately, and all but the forward fuselage was scrapped. It can now be seen at the RAF Manston History Museum.

Seen at RAF Alconbury in August 1982 is Nimrod MR.2 XV230. First flying in 1969, at 1343hrs on 2 September 2006, this aircraft took off from Seeb Airport in Oman for operations over Afghanistan. Shortly after refuelling in the air, a bomb bay fire warning occurred and, 16 minutes later, radio contact was lost, the Nimrod having exploded just over 12 miles west of Kandahar. Sadly, all 14 on board, most of whom came from 120 Sqn, lost their lives.

Nimrod MR.2 XV233 is at RAF Alconbury in July 1984, seen here with 42 Sqn. Built as an MR.1 in 1968, it would become a Nimrod MRA.4 with the serial ZJ520. It was scrapped in February 2011.

Overhead RAF St Mawgan in August 1986 is Nimrod MR.2 XV253. In 2009, it was scrapped at Woodford.

Nimrod MR.1 XV244 of 42 Sqn is at RAF Brize Norton in June 1982. Arriving at RAF Kinloss in November 1970, its conversion to an MR.2 was completed in November 1984. In December 1990, this aircraft left RAF St Mawgan to take part in Operation *Granby*, earning the distinction of being the most successful aircraft and crew, being credited with six kills and one probable and earning the nickname 'Battlestar 42'. It last flew in July 2009 and was subsequently used for spares. It was formally withdrawn from service in March 2010, and, two years later, it was purchased by Morayvia and based at RAF Kinloss, where it remains, having since acquired the name *Duke of Edinburgh*. Note the two squadron shields on the nose.

Nimrod MR.1 XV262 is seen at RAF St Mawgan in August 1980. Built in 1972, it was converted to be a Nimrod AEW.3, only to be scrapped in 1992.

In June 1978, Nimrod MR.1 XV262 is seen overhead RAF St Mawgan.

An ungainly sight overhead RAF Greenham Common in June 1981 was this Nimrod AEW.3, believed to be XZ286.

Nimrod R.1 XW664 is seen at RAF Akrotiri in November 1978. One of three R.1s that only flew with 51 Sqn, its last operational duties were during operations *Ellamy* and *Unified Protector* in Libya between May and June 2011. Its last flight was from RAF Waddington to East Midlands Airport on 12 July 2011, and it can now be seen at the East Midlands Aero Park.

Above: Nimrod MR.1 XV253 is photographed at Gibraltar. It was converted to an MR.2 and then became MRA.4 ZJ525, only to be scrapped at Woodford in 2009, when the MRA.4 programme was cancelled.

Below left and below right: Displaying over RNAS Yeovilton in July 1982 is Nimrod MR.2 XV239, which at this time was based at RAF Kinloss. On 23 August 1995, this aircraft, now with 120 Sqn, deployed to Canada for a series of air displays. On 2 September 1995, it took off from Toronto Pearson International Airport, but during its display sequence, it crashed into Lake Ontario, sadly killing all seven on board. Note the AIM9L Sidewinder missiles under the wings, which were a fitment for self-defence during the Falklands War.

Nimrod AEW.3 XV263, seen with the Joint Trials Unit (JTU) at RAF Abingdon in September 1986, started life as an MR.1. It was converted to an AEW.3 and flew with the JTU based at RAF Waddington; however, following the cancellation of the programme, it was scrapped at Brough in 2011. The fuselage, which was used for fatigue testing the MRA.4 wing, is believed to have survived.

Nimrod MR.1 XV235, seen here at RAF Waddington in June 1980, was quite a well-known aircraft, as it was this aircraft that rendezvoused with the submarines HMS *Trenchant* and USS *Spadefish* at the North Pole in 1992. By then, it had been converted to an MR.2, and, on 5 November 2007, it suffered a fuel leak but avoided the same fate as XV230, which had been lost on 2 September 2006. Retired in March 2010, it was scrapped at RAF Kinloss, but the forward fuselage was saved and can now be seen at the Avro Museum at Woodford.

Nimrod AEW.3 XZ286 rolled out from the factory at Woodford in April 1980, first flew in July 1980 and was seen at the Farnborough Airshow later the same year. It is seen here landing at RAF Greenham Common in June 1981. It would be scrapped at RAF Abingdon in 1991, and its fuselage was used by RAF Kinloss for ground instruction, later being scrapped in 1999.

Seen surrounded by C-130 Hercules aircraft at RAF Lyneham in September 1977 is Nimrod MR.1 XV246. Converted to an MR.2, it was intended to become Nimrod MRA.4 ZJ525, but it was ultimately deemed unsuitable for conversion and scrapped at Woodford in January 2011.

Nimrod MR.2 XV234, seen here at RAF St Mawgan in August 1975, would become Nimrod MRA.4 ZJ518 and first flew in December 2004. Its last flight was March 2010, and, by March 2011, it had been scrapped.

Nimrods rarely belonged to one squadron (apart from 203 Sqn, which was based in Malta), but this 42 Sqn badge is seen on Nimrod MR.1 XZ285 at RAF Finningley in 1977 for the Queen's Jubilee Review. This aircraft would become an MR.2 and then an AEW.3 and was scrapped at RAF Abingdon in 1992.

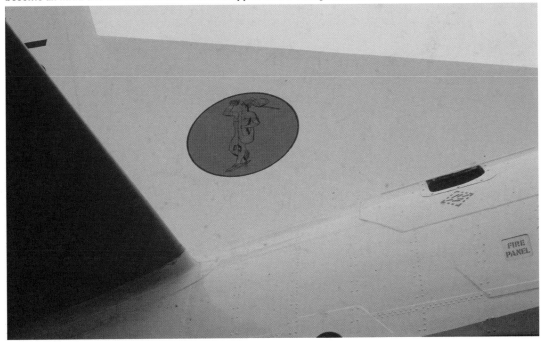

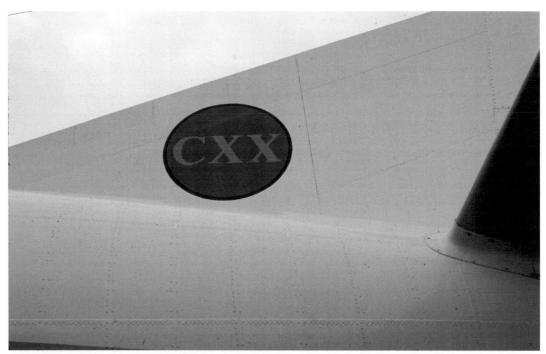

Nimrod MR.1 XV254, also seen at RAF Finningley in July 1977, carries the 120 Sqn badge. Converted to an MR.2, it was retired in March 2010 and scrapped at RAF Kinloss four months later. The forward fuselage was saved for the Highland Aviation Museum, but when this closed in 2019, it was put up for sale. It finally arrived at its new home, the South Wales Aviation Museum, in February 2021.

Nimrod MR.1 XV250 also took park in the Jubilee Review, but with the markings of 201 Sqn on the tail. This aircraft first flew in January 1971 and was delivered to RAF Kinloss the following month. A year later, it was transferred to 203 Sqn at RAF Luqa, returning to RAF Kinloss in 1975. Its conversion to MR.2 was completed by July 1983, and it was withdrawn from RAF service on 31 March 2010. It then flew to the Yorkshire Air Museum on 13 April 2010, where it is maintained in ground operational condition.

The 201 Sqn badge is seen on the tail of XV250 in July 1977.

203 Sqn's badge is seen on the tail of Nimrod MR.1 XV249 at RAF Finningley in July 1977. This aircraft was delivered to RAF Kinloss in February 1971. Converted to an MR.2 in 1985, it was withdrawn from service in 1992 and placed into storage. However, following the ditching of Nimrod R.1 XW666 on 16 May 1995, XV249 was modified to be an R.1 and delivered to 51 Sqn at RAF Waddington in December 1996. It was destined to be the last Nimrod to fly when, on 29 July 2011, it flew from RAF Waddington to Cotswold Airport at Kemble in Gloucestershire where it was dismantled and moved by road to the RAF Museum at Cosford, where it still can be seen today.

The final badge to be seen on a Nimrod MR.1 at RAF Finningley in July 1977 was that of 206 Sqn on XV259. This aircraft was later converted to be an AEW.3, but following the project's cancellation, it was sold in 1991 and then broken up in 1998. The nose was purchased privately in 1998 and went to the Solway Aviation Museum, Carlisle, but is now in private hands.

Nimrod MR.1 XZ282, seen here at RAF St Athan in September 1977, was delivered in 1975 and later converted to an MR.2 and then an AEW.3. It was then scrapped in Scotland in 1996. It carries the 203 Sqn badge on the tail.

Nimrod MR.1 XV242 is overhead RAF Greenham Common in May 1980. Delivered in 1969, it was converted to an MR.2 and then became MRA.4 ZJ517, first flying in this configuration in August 2005, only to be scrapped in 2011 when the project was cancelled.

Nimrod MR.1 XZ282 is getting airborne from Farnborough in 1976. It was scrapped in 1996, having been converted first to an MR.2 and later to an AEW.3.

Nimrod AEW.3 XZ286 is seen at Farnborough in 1980.

Nimrod MR.2 XV226 is overhead RAF Greenham Common in June 1981. This aircraft was the first MR.1 to be built, first flying in June 1968, and was then retained by the manufacturer for trials that included conversion to MR.2. In April 2010, it was flown to Bruntingthorpe in Leicestershire to join the Cold War Collection, where it performed fast taxi runs. Following damage by high winds in 2015, it languished at Bruntingthorpe until all aviation-related activities ceased in March 2020. XV226 has now been moved to a dispersal on the airfield, and its future fate is not known.

Nimrod MR.2 XV255 is seen at RAF Boscombe Down in June 1990. Just under 20 years after this photograph was taken, this aircraft was flown from RAF Kinloss to Norwich Airport and can still be seen at the City of Norwich Aviation Museum at Horsham St Faith.

Hawker Siddeley/BAE Nimrod Variants

Nimrod MR.1
Built for a maritime reconnaissance role. Forty-six were built in total.

Nimrod R.1
Employed in a signal intelligence role. Three were built, and an additional one was converted from an MR.2.

Nimrod MR.2
A modernised MR.1. The suffix 'P' was added to aircraft that had been fitted with air-to-air refuelling equipment. Thirty-five were built in total.

Nimrod AEW.3
Designed for an AEW role. Eleven were converted from MR.1 and MR.2 aircraft, but only three were completed, being flown by the JTU from December 1984. The project was cancelled in 1986.

Nimrod MRA.4
Maritime reconnaissance and attack aircraft. Five were converted from MR.2s. The project was cancelled in 2010.

Nimrod RAF Operational Squadrons

Squadron	Years Active During 1970–89
42 Sqn (42 (R) Sqn from 1992)	from 1971 (disbanded 2010)
51 Sqn	from 1974 (disbanded 2011)
120 Sqn	from 1971 (disbanded 2010)
201 Sqn	from 1970 (disbanded 2010)
203 Sqn	1971–77
206 Sqn	from 1970 (disbanded 2005)
236 OCU	served throughout (disbanded 1992)

Chapter 4
Shackleton

Photographed 18 May 1955 as an indication of the new Coastal Command colours, Lockheed Neptune MR.1 WX547 of 37 Sqn, Sunderland GR.V SZ575 of 201 Sqn and, between them, Shackleton MR.1 VP262 of 120 Sqn. Neptune WX547 suffered an undercarriage collapse at RAF Luqa on 13 January 1956, after which it was written off and was later pushed into the sea off Hal Far, Malta, to be used for underwater film scenes. Sunderland SZ575 had joined 201 Sqn in February 1955 and was struck off charge in October 1957. Shackleton VP262 first flew in February 1951 and joined 120 Sqn in May of the same year. It went into storage in September 1958, was broken up in 1962 and its remains were sold as scrap the following year.

An unidentified Shackleton MR.2 is seen at what appears to be an overseas base, possibly RAF Khormaksar, Aden. If this is correct, this aircraft is possibly from 37 Sqn, to which it was attached in 1967–68.

The Shackleton MR.3 (seen here) together with the MR.2 carried out maritime reconnaissance and search and rescue roles until 1972, when 12 MR.2s were then converted to be the AEW.2. The AEW role was performed solely by 8 Sqn until June 1991.

Shackleton MR.2 WR955 first flew in November 1955 and subsequently flew with 224, 120, 210, 204 and 42 Sqns. It finally went to A&AEE in Boscombe Down in March 1971, where it was used for trials in connection with the conversion to the AEW.2. When the trials were complete, it went to RAF Brize Norton for fire-fighting training, this photograph being taken in 1976–78. Its remains were later scrapped.

On the top of the fuselage of Shackleton AEW.2 WR960 of 8 Sqn is the Orange Harvest electronic support measures 'spark plug' antenna. This aircraft first flew in February 1954 as an MR.2, subsequently flying with 228, 210 and 205 Sqns. In May 1971, conversion to an AEW.2 started, after which it went to 8 Sqn in June 1972. It then went to RAF Cosford in November 1982 for ground instructional duties but, in January 1983, went to the Air and Space Hall of the Museum of Science and Industry in Manchester. This Hall has recently closed, and it is expected WR960 will go to the Avro Heritage Museum at Woodford. 8 Sqn's Shackletons were named after characters from the children's TV programme *The Magic Roundabout*, this aircraft being named *Dougal*.

Shackleton MR.2 WL801 first flew in October 1953, after which it flew with 38, 42 and 8 Sqns. It was used by 8 Sqn for crew training until its fatigue life was expended; its last flight was to RAF Cosford on 11 June 1976, where it was then used as a ground instructional airframe. It then went to the Cosford Aerospace Museum but was subsequently scrapped.

Shackleton AEW.2 WL757 of 8 Sqn is seen at RAF Brize Norton in October 1990; this squadron was the only one to fly this variant. First flown in April 1953 as an MR.2, it served with 37, 38, 204 and 205 Sqns and was converted to an AEW.2 in 1971, being delivered to 8 Sqn in August 1972. It was retired in March 1989 and is currently deteriorating at Paphos Airport, Cyprus. This aircraft was named *Brian*.

The tail of Shackleton AEW.2 WL756, seen here at RNAS Yeovilton in September 1984, has received a number of 'zaps'. First flying in April 1953, its last flight was to RAF St Mawgan in June 1991; it ended up on the fire dump and was scrapped in 1999, but the nose section survived and was last reported as being in private hands in Holland. This aircraft was named *Mr Rusty*.

Shacketon MR.3 WR977 was delivered to 220 Sqn in October 1957 and then 201 Sqn when 220 Sqn was renumbered in October 1958. It then served with 206, 201, 42 and 203 Sqns, and, in November 1971, it was given to RAF Thorney Island for practice firefighting; however, it immediately went to RAF Finingley and was earmarked again for scrapping. In 1977, the aircraft was moved to Newark Air Museum, where this photograph was taken, in July 1991. It is still at the museum today.

Seen at RNAS Yeovilton, in July 1982, is Shackleton AEW.2 WR960. First flown in February 1954 as an MR.2, conversion to an AEW.2 started in May 1971, after which it went to 8 Sqn. It then went to RAF Cosford in November 1982 for ground instructional duties, after which it went to the Manchester Science and Industry Museum. It is now expected to go to the Avro Heritage Museum.

A close-up of WR960's tail, taken at RAF Mildenhall in May 1982.

The other end – the nose of WR960 showing the 8 Sqn badge and squadron commander's pennant, the commanding officer at that time being Wing Commander (Wg Cdr) David Greenway OBE, who had taken over from Wg Cdr Bill Newman five days before this photograph was taken.

WR960 is nose-on and showing the radar housing and the bomb-aimer's position.

Seen at RAF Cosford in May 1982, where it was being used for ground instruction, is Shackleton MR.2 WL801, which first flew in October 1953. Its last flight was to RAF Cosford on 11 June 1976, after which it then went to the Cosford Aerospace Museum but was subsequently scrapped.

Also seen at RAF Cosford in May 1982 was Shackleton MR.3 WR974. First flown in January 1957, after trial and evaluation work, it was delivered to 203 Sqn in February 1958, after which it was used for further trials work from 1964 to 1968, before flying with 203 and 42 Sqns and eventually going to RAF Cosford. It was put up for sale in 1988, after which it went to the Gatwick Aviation Museum. In 2014, it went to Bruntingthorpe but in 2020 moved to the South Wales Air Museum at St Athan.

Overhead RAF Abingdon in September 1983 is Shackleton AEW.2 WL790. First flown as an MR.2 in June 1953, it flew with 204, 269, 210 and 205 Sqns before being converted to an AEW.2 and joining 8 Sqn in September 1972. It last flew with the RAF in July 1991, before joining the Shackleton Preservation Trust at Coventry Airport. However, in 1994, it flew to the US and continued to fly until 2009, after which it went to the Pima Air & Space Museum at Tucson, Arizona, where it still is today. This aircraft was named *Mr McHenry*.

Seen overhead RAF Waddington in June 1980 is Shackleton AEW.2. First flown in March 1952, this MR.2 served on 37, 42 and 204 Sqns before being converted to be an AEW.2. Its flying career ended in January 1981, when it was sent to RAF Valley for crash rescue and fire practice. Apparently, it was displayed rather than destroyed, but it was eventually scrapped in 1987. This aircraft carried the name *Paul*.

Photographed at RAF St Mawgan in August 1980 is Shackleton AEW.2 WL741. First flown in December 1952, it flew with 224, 42 and 205 Sqn before being converted to an AEW.2, after which it was given the name *PC Knapweed*. Withdrawn from use in 1981, it was flown to RAF Manston and later burned.

Seen at RAF Changi, Singapore, is a Shackleton MR.2C of 205 Sqn. This squadron converted to the MR.2C in February 1962 and was disbanded in October 1971.

Above, left and below: Seen overhead RAF Greenham Common in June 1981 is Shackleton AEW.2 WR965. First flown in April 1954, it flew with 37, 203, 205 and 204 Sqns and was converted to an AEW.2, joining 8 Sqn in January 1973 where it was given the name *Dill*. On 30 April 1990, it was taking part in a maritime exercise off Benbecula, but, at 1037hrs, it inexplicably struck the ground 30ft below the summit of an 823ft hill on the Isle of Harris. Sadly, all ten crew lost their lives.

Shackleton MR.2 WL738 ended its days as a gate guardian at RAF Lossiemouth from 1978, until it was scrapped in 1991. First flown in November 1952, it flew with 204, 37, 210 and 204 Sqns; it joined 8 Sqn in March 1974 for pilot training but was struck off charge in October 1977, having used up its fatigue life. It was then used for spares recovery before going on display at the main gate.

Getting airborne from RAF Luqa in Malta in July 1978 is Shackleton AEW.2 WR963, which carried the name *Ermintrude*. First flown in March 1954, it served with 224, 210, 38 and 205 Sqns before being converted to at AEW.2. Its end of service came in July 1991, when it was flown to Coventry Airport. It is currently owned by the Shackleton Aviation Group.

Another Shackleton AEW.2 getting airborne from RAF Luqa in July 1978 was WL793. First flown as an MR.2 in July 1953, it flew with 38, 204 and 210 Sqns before joining 8 Sqn as an AEW.2 in February 1973, where it too was given the name *Ermintrude*. It was grounded in 1981, after which it was used for battle damage repair but was soon towed to the fire dump. By July 1982, it was all but destroyed and its remains cut up for scrap.

Photographed in November 1973 is a brightly coloured Shackleton T.4 VP293. Built as an MR.1, it first flew in July 1951, after which it served with 224, 42 and 206 Sqns before being converted to a T.4 between 1956 and 1958. It then flew with the RAE and A&AEE, as well as the Maritime Operational Training Unit at RAF Kinloss. Struck off charge after being with the RAE in 1975, it went to the Strathallen Museum (where this photograph was taken) but was broken up in 1996, although the nose section was saved.

With all engines running, Shackleton AEW.2 WR963 prepares to take off from RAF Greenham Common in June 1979.

On static display at RAF Greenham Common in June 1979 was the ill-fated Shackleton AEW.2 WR965, which would be destroyed in an accident on 30 April 1990.

Seen at RAF Greenham Common in May 1980 was Shackleton AEW.2 WL747. First flown in February 1953, it served as an MR.2 with 204, 42, 37 and 210 Sqns before being converted to an AEW.2 and arriving at 8 Sqn in April 1972, where it was given the name *Florence*. In July 1991, it was flown to Paphos Airport in Cyprus, where its remains still languish.

Seen at RAF Greenham Common in August 1976 is Shackleton AEW.2 WL795. First flown in August 1953, it flew with 204, 269, 210, 38 and 205 Sqns before being converted to an AEW.2 and arriving on 8 Sqn in October 1972, where it was given the name *Rosalie*. It was withdrawn from operational flying in 1981 and then given to RAF St Mawgan for crash rescue and fire practice. At some stage, it was at the Cornish Aviation Heritage Centre and the subject of an unsuccessful restoration appeal; it now sits at Cornwall Airport Newquay, adjacent to the heritage centre.

Seen on the starboard fins of WL795 are unofficial 'zaps'.

Awaiting its fate at RAF Kemble in February 1977 is Shackleton MR.2 WR961. First flown in February 1954, it served with 228, 224, 204, 37 and 38 Sqns, finally finishing with 204 Sqn. It went into storage at Kemble in April 1972 and was scrapped a year after this photograph was taken.

Photographed at RAF Finningley on 29 July 1977 as part of the Air Defence formation during the Queen's Jubilee Review was Shackleton AEW.2 WL756. *Mr Rusty* was scrapped in 1999, but the nose section survived and was last reported as being in private hands in Holland.

Above and below: Seen overhead RAF Lossiemouth is Shackleton AEW.2 WL793. *Ermintrude* was grounded in 1981, after which it was used for battle damage repair but was soon towed to the fire dump and was all but destroyed and its remains cut up for scrap.

Evidence of *The Magic Roundabout* connection with Shackletons is this *Mr Rusty* badge, which identifies the aircraft as Shackleton AEW.2 WL756 when it is seen at RAF St Mawgan.

Avro Shackleton Operational Variants
Shackleton MR.1
Maritime reconnaissance aircraft. Twenty-nine were built in total.

Shackleton MR.1A
Maritime reconnaissance aircraft powered by Griffon 57A engine. Forty-seven were built and surviving MR.1s were converted.

Shackleton MR.2
Maritime reconnaissance aircraft. There were 69 built in total.

Shackleton MR.3
The maritime Reconnaissance and anti-shipping variant. Thirty-four were built in total.

Shackleton AEW.2
Airborne early warning aircraft. Twelve were converted from MR.2 specification.

Shackleton RAF Operational Squadrons
Note: Some squadrons began or ended their use of the Shackleton outside the scope of this book. As such, the years served within the time frame have been listed.

Squadron	Years Active During 1970–89
8 Sqn	from 1972 (disbanded 1991)
42 Sqn	until Sep 1971
120 Sqn	until Feb 1971
201 Sqn	until Dec 1970
203 Sqn	until Dec 1971
204 Sqn	until May 1972
205 Sqn	until Oct 1971
206 Sqn	until Oct 1970
210 Sqn	until Nov 1971
Maritime Operational Training Unit	until 1970